Clexit for a Bright Future

The Case for Withdrawing from
United Nations' Climate Treaties

D0967283

Dears, Donn D.

Clexit for a Bright Future: The Case for Withdrawing from United Nations' Climate Treaties

Includes Index

1. Greenhouse Gases

2. CO2 Emissions

3. Storage of Electricity

4. UNFCCC Treaty

5. Fossil Fuels

ISBN 978-0-9815119-3-1

Published by Critical Thinking Press

Cover Design by Kevin Leonard

Manufactured in the United States

© 2017 by Donn Dears

Dedicated to:

Marion, the love of my life, who is missed beyond belief.

Table of Contents

Chapter   Page

Preface   1

Foreword   5

1 The UNFCCC   7

2 Worldwide CO2 Emissions   13

3 Cutting U.S. CO2 Emissions 80% 19

4 Cutting U.S. Gasoline Use 80% 25

5 Comments on the UNFCCC Treaty 31

Appendix 1: Carbon Capture and Sequestration 37

Appendix 2: Alternative Uses of CO2 41

Appendix 3: Storage   45

Appendix 4: Decline of Nuclear Power in the United States 47

Appendix 5: Text of UNFCCC Treaty 51

Notes   93

About the Author   97

Index   99

Figures
		Page
Figure 1	CO2 Emissions 2014 – 2030	17
Figure 2	Tesla Vehicle	26
Figure 3	Graph of Nuclear Generation	48

Tables
Table 1	CO2 Emissions by Major Country	14
Table 2	U.S. CO2 Emissions	15
Table 3	Installed Generating Capacity by Type	21
Table 4	Remaining U.S. CO2 Emissions	28

Preface

By Bryan Leyland, New Zealand

The Paris Agreement on climate change is nonsense and, if the United States stands by the commitment made by Barrack Obama, it will cost the country billions of dollars, increase the price of electricity, reduce the reliability of the power system, and do virtually nothing to slow down (mythical) dangerous, man-made global warming.

In his book *Clexit for a Bright Future*, Donn Dears sets out very clearly why the accord is nonsense and why it would seriously damage the U.S. economy. "Clexit" is the only rational option.

Dears exposes the farcical nature of the Paris Agreement negotiated at the 21st Conference of the Parties (COP 21) of the United Nations Framework Convention on Climate Change (UNFCCC): It doesn't specify the amount of greenhouse gas reduction or have any enforcement mechanisms.

Dears also, quite rightly, points out that there is no substantial scientific evidence supporting the hypothesis that man-made greenhouse gases cause dangerous global warming. He further notes that, even if they did, the enormous effort and expenditure that the United States—and the world—would incur to reduce carbon dioxide emissions by a substantial amount would make virtually no difference to the world's climate.

It is foolish for the United States to embark on an exercise in futility that will devastate its economy while ignoring the fact that China and India alone plan to add more fossil-fuel energy

Preface

generation and carbon dioxide emissions than currently exist in America. The world and the environment would be far better off if the United States spent the money helping to provide electricity, clean water, and sewage treatment to developing countries.

Dears points out that electricity generation is the lifeblood of the economy, and, with gasoline, makes up 60 percent of U.S. carbon dioxide emissions. Wind and solar power are 8 percent of the installed capacity, but only provide about 5 percent of the nation's energy. In addition, those sources often provide very little power during maximum demand periods, and the shortfall is made up via inefficient, quick-response gas turbines that emit large quantities of carbon dioxide. In short: wind and solar power are very expensive and do very little to reduce carbon dioxide emissions. Nuclear power, by contrast, is safe, cheaper and better—violently opposed by the environmentalists.

Dears also analyses the contribution that electric cars and fuel cells could make to reducing emissions. He concludes that electric cars can't make a big difference, and it is possible that fuel cells could actually increase emissions.

Plentiful low-cost energy has freed the developed world from starvation, disease and misery. As a result, the average person in the developed world now lives better than a king did a few hundred years ago. Constraining the availability of low-cost energy from fossil fuels will ensure that billions of people in the developing world will continue to face starvation, disease and misery.

The book is a valuable contribution to the growing evidence that dangerous man-made global warming is the biggest hoax in the history of the world—and that futile efforts to solve this non-

Preface

existent problem will impoverish billions of people in the United States and all over the world. Is that what we want?

The United States has an opportunity to exit the UNFCCC treaty and lead the world into re-establishing honest science as the basis for policies—and, if necessary, actions regarding climate change.

Bryan Leyland
New Zealand-based consulting engineer

Bryan has Masters degree in power system design and is a Fellow of the Institution of Professional Engineers, New Zealand, the Institution of Mechanical Engineers (UK) and a retired Fellow of the Institution of Engineering and Technology (UK).

Foreword

Clexit For a Bright Future is a sequel to *Nothing to Fear*.

Clexit establishes why the United States should withdraw from the United Nations Framework Convention on Climate Change (UNFCCC) treaty.

It provides the facts that show it is impossible to cut carbon dioxide (CO2) and other greenhouse gas (GHG) emissions enough to slow or stop climate change. It demonstrates that the UNFCCC treaty cannot achieve its stated purpose:

> The ultimate objective of this Convention and any related legal instruments that the Conference of the Parties may adopt is to achieve, in accordance with the relevant provisions of the Convention, stabilization of greenhouse gas concentrations in the atmosphere at a level that would prevent dangerous anthropogenic interference with the climate system. Such a level should be achieved within a time-frame sufficient to allow ecosystems to adapt naturally to climate change, to ensure that food production is not threatened and to enable economic development to proceed in a sustainable manner.

Perpetuating a failed treaty is immoral.

Money spent trying to achieve an impossible objective should be spent instead on improving the lives of people.

Chapter 1

The UNFCCC

The United Nations Framework Convention on Climate Change (UNFCCC) treaty was ratified by the U.S. Senate in 1992.

Every year since then, the member countries of the UNFCCC have conducted meetings, referred to as Conferences of the Parties, or COPs, where steps were taken to have countries cut their carbon dioxide (CO2) emissions. The premise has been that atmospheric CO2 is the cause of global warming and climate change.

The twenty-first UNFCCC meeting, COP 21, held in Paris from November 30 through December 12, 2015, finally reached an agreement where the world would attempt to cut CO2 emissions enough to prevent a temperature rise greater than 2 degrees C. Atmospheric CO2 levels under the agreement were not to exceed 450 ppm. Currently, they are 400 ppm.

President Barack Obama signed the agreement for the United States even though the Senate had not ratified it as a treaty.

As of, January 18, 2017, 125 of the 197 signatories have ratified the agreement. The agreement went into force on November 4, 2016, when 55 countries, representing at least 55% of worldwide CO2 emissions, ratified the agreement. As with the Kyoto protocol, a new governing mechanism has been put in place, known as the CMA, or "Conference of the Parties to the Convention serving as the meeting of the Parties to the Paris Agreement.[1]"

There is in fact a bureaucratic structure within the UNFCCC, including the Subsidiary Body for Implementation (SBI) and the Subsidiary Body for Scientific and Technological Advice (SBSTA).[2]

There are, however, two huge problems with the COP 21 agreement, beside the problem of whether the United States has adopted COP 21 as a treaty:

> First, there is substantial evidence that CO_2 is not the primary cause of global warming and climate change.

> Second, it's impossible for the world to cut CO_2 emissions enough to slow or stop climate change, if CO_2 is actually the problem.

While the first problem is a question for science to answer, there should be no doubt about the second problem.

And it's the second problem that needs to be understood, because if we can't slow or stop climate change, our time and energy and tax dollars would be better spent finding ways to adjust to it.

In addition, the COP 21 agreement is largely a sham, because it doesn't stipulate how much CO_2 emissions must be cut and contains no enforcement mechanisms.

The Economist magazine made this clear when it reported:

> Each country is to set its own goals, called "Intended Nationally Determined Contributions" (INDCs), but there is little expectation that these INDCs will add up to enough reductions in CO_2 to stop global warming.[3]

The UNFCCC

The reality is, "In order to stabilize CO_2 concentrations at about 450 ppm by 2050, global emissions would have to decline by about 60% by 2050. Industrialized countries' [sic] greenhouse gas emissions would have to decline by about 80% by 2050.[4]" Others say that CO_2 emissions must be cut to zero by 2070 to prevent a climate disaster.[5]

There seems to be substantial agreement that CO_2 emissions must be cut worldwide 50%. For example, *National Geographic* reported that CO_2 emissions must be cut 50 to 80% by 2050.[6]

President Obama and the EPA have declared the United States must cut its CO_2 emissions 80% by 2050.[7]

There have been attempts in Congress to establish these required cuts into law. For example, the Global Warming Pollution Reduction Act of 2007, to cut CO_2 emissions 80% by 2050, was proposed, but not passed by the U.S. Senate.

Accordingly, the benchmarks set by global warming true believers for cutting CO_2 emissions to prevent a climate catastrophe are:

- The world must cut CO_2 emissions 50% by 2050.
- The United States must cut its CO_2 emissions 80% by 2050.

Whether these cuts are achievable should be the metric used to determine whether the United States should withdraw from the UNFCCC treaty.

If it's impossible for the world to cut CO_2 emissions 50%, or for the United States or other developed countries to cut their CO_2 emissions 80%, the UNFCCC treaty is essentially a fraud.

The UNFCCC

If these goals are impossible to meet, the United States should withdraw from the UNFCCC treaty.

Efforts to cut CO_2 emissions by 50% or 80% would do great economic harm, and if these efforts can't stop the climate catastrophe their advocates predict, then it would be unethical to continue to impose regulations and laws to force CO_2 reductions.

The Economist magazine was touching on an important issue in its description of why COP 21 wasn't addressing how much CO_2 emissions needed to be cut.

COP meetings would continue to take place year after year if the UNFCCC won't face up to whether CO_2 emissions can be cut enough to stop the climate catastrophe that CO_2 is supposedly causing.

Every year, tens of thousands of people from 197 countries would continue to assemble at huge expense at COP meetings. And every year additional thousands would attend the other UNFCCC functions, such as the SBI and SBSTA meetings.

Billions of dollars would be wasted on a perpetually failing endeavor known as the UNFCCC.

And this money would pale in comparison to the money spent on useless attempts to cut CO_2 emissions.

By one account, over $100 billion has been spent by the United States on efforts to cut CO_2 emissions.[8]

The Federal Climate Change Expenditures Report to Congress showed a 2014 budget of $21 billion for efforts to cut CO_2 emissions, with two prior year budgets over $19 billion.[9]

The UNFCCC

Germany has spent over $20 billion each year over the past several years on its efforts to cut CO_2 emissions.[10]

These billions of dollars could have been spent on improving infrastructure, or for improving the living conditions of people in developing countries.

Can worldwide CO_2 emissions be cut 50% by 2050?

Can U.S. CO_2 emissions be cut 80% by 2050?

These are the real issues, and the next few chapters will explain why it's impossible to achieve either target.

Chapter 2

Worldwide CO2 Emissions

Can CO2 emissions be cut 50% worldwide by 2050, or will there be a climate catastrophe?

This 50% requirement is based on the assumption that atmospheric CO2 must be kept below 450 ppm, where atmospheric CO2 is currently 400 ppm.

Computer models predict that temperatures could rise as much as 8 degrees F if these last 50 ppm are allowed to happen.

What are the facts?

What are the CO2 emissions of the major countries in the world?

Table 1 shows CO2 emissions for 2014 for the major economies of the world.

These six countries account for 70% of CO2 emissions worldwide.

Realistically, only two sources of CO2 emissions are relevant to any attempt to cut CO2 emissions.

They are:

- Generation of electricity
- Gasoline use

Industrial causes are too diverse for effective action. They include cement production, natural gas for heat treating and heating, etc.

Worldwide CO2 Emissions

While Table 2 is for the United States only, Europe and Russia have similar distributions of CO2 emissions. China and India, the two largest developing countries, have more emissions from the generation of electricity than from gasoline use.

How will it be possible to cut CO2 emissions 80% from the generation of electricity and the use of gasoline?

Table 1 CO2 Emissions by Major Country			
Country	CO2 emissions (MMT)	Per capita emissions (Tons)	% of Total World
World	35,270	-	
China	10,300	7.4	29.2%
United States	5,300	16.6	15.0%
EU28	3,400	6.8	9.6%
India	2,500	1.9	7.1%
Russia	1,800	12.6	5.1%
Japan	1,400	10.7	4.0%
			70.0%
Estimates for 2014			

Worldwide CO2 Emissions

Before examining how the United States can cut its CO2 emissions 80% by 2050, one must ask whether such a herculean effort would have any effect on the world's ability to prevent the climate catastrophe predicted by the UNFCCC and Intergovernmental Panel on Climate Change (IPCC), which is the basis for the COP 21 agreement.

Table 2 U.S. CO2 Emissions (2004)[11]		
Source	**MMT**	**% Total**
Electric Generation	2298.6	39%
Gasoline	1162.6	20%
Industrial	1069.3	18%
Transportation (Excluding Gasoline)	771.1	13%
Residential	374.7	6%
Commercial	228.8	4%
United States Total	5905.1	100%
Later data combined gasoline with all transportation.		
Source: *Emission of Greenhouse Gases in the United States 2005* by DOE Energy Information Administration. MMT = Million Metric Tons		

Worldwide CO2 Emissions

What are the facts?

1. China and India already emit more CO2 than does the United States, EU28, Russia and Japan combined.

2. China and India are developing countries that will be allowed by the Paris Accord to increase their CO2 emissions.

3. The UN has said the world must cut total CO2 emissions 50% by 2050, which means, referring to Table 1, cutting CO2 emissions by 17,635 MMT.

4. Assuming the United States, Europe, Russia and Japan cut their CO2 emissions 80%, it would amount to only 9,520 MMT, nowhere near the 17,635 MMT needed for the world to prevent a hypothetical climate catastrophe.

5. The remaining developing countries that produce 30% of the world's CO2 emissions are mostly struggling to survive, with countries in Africa and many in Asia barely at subsistence levels. Most of those countries, with the exception of oil-producing countries and South Korea, would be unable to cut CO2 emissions by any amount.

No amount of speech making by 10,000 attendees in Marrakesh at the UN COP 22 climate change conference the week of November 6, 2016, changed these facts.

Referring to Table 1, the United States, Europe, Russia and Japan could completely eliminate their CO2 emissions and it would still not result in cutting worldwide CO2 emissions 50%.

Worldwide CO2 Emissions

Meanwhile China and India are continuing to grow their CO2 emissions.

Figure 1 shows that China's CO2 emissions could reach 17,834 MMT by 2030. An estimate by MIT showed they might only reach 13,000 MMT, but even this lower level exceeds the combined level of current CO2 emissions by the United State, Europe, Russia and Japan.

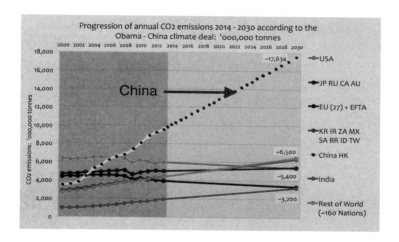

Figure 1
CO2 Emissions 2014 - 2030.
From Watts Up With That by E. Hoskins

It's painfully clear that the world cannot cut CO2 emissions by 50% even if the United States, Europe, Russia and Japan were to cut their CO2 emissions by 100%.

Worldwide CO2 Emissions

Cutting CO2 emissions can't stop climate change even if CO2 emissions are the cause.

This means efforts to cut CO2 emissions are a waste of money, time and effort, and that the money being spent on cutting CO2 emissions can be used to benefit people around the world.

It also means that crippling regulations, such as the efforts by the World Bank to prevent the building of coal-fired power plants in Sub-Saharan Africa, can be abolished so that poor people can get the electricity they need to improve their lives.

McKinsey & Company reported:[12]

> Sub-Saharan Africa is starved for electricity. It has 13% of the world's population, but 48% of the share of global population without access to electricity.

Cutting CO2 emissions to no avail is a crime against humanity.

Chapter 3

Cutting U.S. CO2 emissions 80%

As shown in Chapter 2, it's impossible for the world to cut CO2 emissions enough to prevent a hypothetical climate disaster, but could the United States cut its CO2 emissions 80% by 2050?

As seen in Chapter 2, electricity generation and gasoline use produced 59%, or nearly two-thirds of CO2 emissions in the United States.

These CO2 emissions must be cut 80% from 1990 levels if there is to be any possibility of cutting total U.S. CO2 emissions 80% by 2050, as required by Obama and the EPA.

The percentage of U.S. electricity generation in MWh, and related CO2 emissions in million metric tons (MMT) for each source in 2014, are:

- Coal = 33%   CO2 = **1,364 MMT**

- Natural gas = 33%   CO2 = **530 MMT**

- Nuclear = 20%   CO2 = **0**

- Hydropower = 6%   CO2 = **0**

- Other renewables = 7%   CO2 = **0**

- Oil 1%   CO2 = **24 MMT**

Cutting CO2 emissions 80% from 1990 levels requires that total CO2 emissions from electricity generation in 2050 not exceed **364 MMT**.

Cutting U.S. CO2 emissions 80%

The year 1990 has been considered the base year for measuring reductions in CO2 emissions.[13] CO2 emissions in 1990, from generation of electricity, according to the EPA web site, were 1,821 MMT.

An 80% reduction from 1,821 MMT would require reducing CO2 levels in 2050 to **364 MMT**.

Carbon capture and sequestration (CCS) is not a viable option for eliminating CO2 from the atmosphere. (See Appendix 1) Neither are the proposals to convert CO2 to another substance, such as ethanol. (See Appendix 2)

Without CCS, all coal-fired power plants and one-third of all existing natural gas power plants must be shut down if CO2 emissions are to be kept below **364 MMT**.[14]

Wind and solar as replacements

There are two fundamental reasons why wind and solar can't replace the coal-fired and natural gas power plants that must be closed.

- Wind and solar don't generate electricity when the wind doesn't blow or the sun doesn't shine.

- Solar doesn't generate electricity during nighttime hours.

Currently, there are 1,068,422 MW of installed capacity of all types. See Table 3.

This amount of capacity must be available at all times to provide electricity during periods of peak load.

But 441,704 MW of this capacity, or 41%, is eliminated when all coal-fired and 1/3 of natural gas power plants are shut down, so there won't be sufficient capacity available to respond to peak loads.

Table 3 Installed Generating Capacity by Type (in MW)	
Coal	299,094
Natural gas	432,150
Total Coal & NG	731,244
1/3 of NG	142,610
Total Shutdown (Coal + 1/3 NG)	441,704
Total for all sources	1,068,422
Data from EIA	

Therefore, if wind and solar are used to replace the lost capacity, the remaining installed capacity would be insufficient to meet peak demand when the wind stopped blowing or the sun didn't shine.

This alone means that wind and solar can't replace the lost baseload power that's needed to be available at all times, 24/7, for when the wind doesn't blow and the sun doesn't shine.

The only theoretical possibility for using wind and solar to replace closed coal-fired and natural gas power plants would be to install storage essentially equal to the lost capacity. Unfortunately, there is no type of storage currently available that can store this amount of electricity across all of the United States. (Appendix 3)

In addition, there are economic reasons why wind and solar can't be economically used to replace coal-fired and natural gas power plants.

- The cost of building, at $2,000 per KW, the approximately 588,939 new wind turbines,[15] each rated 2 MW, needed to replace the lost coal-fired and natural gas units would be $1.2 trillion. Using offshore wind would cost approximately twice this amount.

- The cost for using photovoltaic (PV) solar at $3,000 per KW, where capacity factor is 0.2, would be around $2.0 trillion while concentrating solar, at around $5,000 per KW, would cost over $3 trillion.

- The cost of constructing new transmission lines to transport the power from remote areas to where it can be used must be added to the investment in new wind and solar capacity. This investment in new transmission lines could easily exceed $200 billion.[16]

Replacing coal-fired and natural gas power plants with nuclear would allow a transition where CO2 emissions could be cut 80%. But the public has been conditioned to believe nuclear power is dangerous, so there is little likelihood that very many new nuclear power plants will be built. In fact, it's very probable there will be less nuclear power available in 2050 than there is today. (See Appendix 4)

Cutting U.S. CO2 emissions 80%

Even if nuclear were acceptable, it would require building approximately 400 new nuclear plants rated 1,000 MW each by 2050, which would be virtually impossible.[17] Currently, there are about 100 nuclear power plants in the U.S.

Conclusion

It is impossible to eliminate all coal-fired power plants and 1/3 of natural gas power plants by 2050 without destroying America's standard of living by forcing Americans to accept huge reductions in the use of electricity, such as for air conditioning, appliances, communications, wireless technology, television, etc., and without crippling American industry.

Chapter 4

Cutting U.S. Gasoline Use 80%

Referring to Table 2, gasoline produced 20% of U.S. CO2 emissions.

Gasoline and generating electricity, combined, produced 59% of U.S. CO2 emissions.

Chapter 3 established it is impossible to cut CO2 emissions 80% from the generation of electricity.

Is it also impossible to cut the use of gasoline 80% by 2050?

Light vehicles are the primary users of gasoline in the United States. Large vehicles, such as trucks, referred to as 18 wheelers, primarily use diesel fuel.

Can gasoline be replaced with an alternative fuel?

Ethanol was once considered an alternative, but many people agree that ethanol doesn't cut CO2 emissions.[18] Using ethanol produced from corn or other food crops is also unethical.

Only two alternatives have been proposed for eliminating the use of gasoline:

- Battery-powered electric vehicles
- Fuel cells

<u>Electric vehicles</u>

If, as described in Chapter 3, coal-fired and natural gas power plants are closed, there will be insufficient capacity to generate adequate supplies of electricity for everyday use, let alone for battery-powered vehicles.

Cutting U.S. Gasoline Use 80%

Even before eliminating coal-fired and natural gas power plants, existing power generation capacity is insufficient to provide the needed electricity to recharge batteries if all 260 million light vehicles on the road today were powered by batteries.

Figure 2: Tesla battery-powered vehicle

Specifically, the Pacific Northwest National Laboratory (PNNL) determined that existing U.S. generating capacity could meet electricity demand so long as no more than 60% of light vehicles were battery powered. Additional power generation capacity would be required if more than 60% of all light vehicles were battery powered.

There is, therefore, insufficient generating capacity to replace 80% of gasoline vehicles with battery-powered electric vehicles even before eliminating any generating capacity. Generating capacity would be totally inadequate after eliminating 41% of existing power generation capacity.

Cutting U.S. Gasoline Use 80%

If there is insufficient supply of electricity to charge batteries, battery-powered vehicles cannot be used to cut CO_2 emissions from gasoline by 80%.

<u>Fuel cells</u>

Fuel cells require hydrogen for their fuel. Hydrogen is not naturally occurring and must be produced. Hydrogen can be produced from water by using electrolysis. This would not be viable when coal-fired and natural gas power plants are closed.

Hydrogen can be produced from natural gas, i.e., methane, by either steam-methane reforming, which currently produces over 95% of hydrogen, or by a water-gas shift process.

Methane reforming and the water-gas shift process also produce CO_2.

At this point, it's difficult to evaluate whether fuel cell vehicles can displace gasoline-powered vehicles, but there are some obvious obstacles.

- The cost of manufacturing fuel cell vehicles isn't publicized, though fuel cells are estimated to cost several times more than an internal combustion engine.

- The lack of hydrogen fueling stations will require an investment of around $50 billion to build 100,000 hydrogen fueling stations. Currently, there are about 12 hydrogen fueling stations in the U.S. For comparison, there are approximately 160,000 gasoline service stations in the U.S.

- The cost of producing hydrogen by methane reforming will be substantial. It's unknown whether it's better to produce the hydrogen centrally and transport it to service stations with a 25% loss of hydrogen during cryogenic transport, or whether it's better to produce hydrogen at the fueling station where costs will be greater due to lost economies of scale.

Table 4 Remaining U.S. CO2 Emissions (2004)		
Source	**MMT**	**% Total**
1. Industrial	1069.3	18%
2. Transportation (Excluding Gasoline)	771.1	13%
3. Residential & Commercial	603.5	10%
Source: Energy Information Administration		

- It's unknown whether consumers will accept fuel cell vehicles, where space is required for cylinders rated 10,000 psi for hydrogen storage. Manufacturers are now building a very limited number of fuel cell vehicles, so some experience will be gained regarding consumer acceptance over the next decade.

- It's unknown whether the CO_2 produced from the reforming process will significantly add to the difficulty of cutting CO_2 emissions 80%.

- It's questionable whether fuel cell vehicles, which are still experimental, can be built and sold in sufficient quantities over the next 30 years to eliminate 80% of light vehicles by 2050. There are approximately 260 million light vehicles in the United States today, and approximately 208 million will have to be replaced with fuel cell vehicles by 2050.

Summary

- Battery-powered vehicles cannot be used to eliminate 80% of gasoline by 2050.

- While not impossible, it's very unlikely that over 200 million fuel cell vehicles will be sold by 2050. Without these fuel cell vehicles, it will be impossible to cut CO_2 emissions from gasoline use 80% by 2050.

Remaining Sources of CO2

Table 4 shows the remaining sources of CO_2 in the United States.

1. Natural gas is the primary source of CO_2 emissions from industrial processes, such as producing cement and heat treating. These and similar processes require high temperatures that are best achieved with natural gas. Electricity can be used as an alternative in some situations, but electricity, as shown in the preceding chapter, will not

be available. Natural gas is also used in the production of chemicals.

2. Diesel and jet fuels are the primary fuels used by the transportation sector, other than gasoline. As established in *Nothing to Fear*,[19] biofuels are not a viable alternative to diesel or jet fuels.

3. Heating is the predominant use of natural gas in the residential and commercial segments.

It will be virtually impossible to cut CO2 emissions 80% from the remaining segments by 2050.

Chapter 5

Comments on the UNFCCC Treaty

Dracula sucked the life blood from his victims, and it required a stake through the heart to kill him.

Like Dracula, the UNFCCC treaty will drain the life blood from the United States, and like Dracula, it must be destroyed with a stake through its heart. Withdrawing from the UNFCCC treaty would be that stake.

As shown in Chapters 2 and 3 it's impossible to cut CO_2 emissions in the United States 80% by 2050 without destroying America's standard of living.

It means cutting per-capita emissions from 16.6 tons to 2.3 tons. The year 1900 was the last time per-capita CO_2 emissions were that low in the United States.

America is best served by abandoning efforts to cut CO_2 emissions and by withdrawing from the UNFCCC treaty.

Chapter 2 demonstrated it is impossible for the world to cut CO_2 emissions by 50%, so the UNFCCC treaty cannot achieve the purpose for which it was intended.

It makes no sense to continue with the charade, in the form of the UNFCCC treaty that can't prevent a hypothetical climate disaster and that will consume huge quantities of financial resources that could otherwise be used to build infrastructure for making people's lives better around the world.

The United States has one vote out of 197, where many of the countries are hostile to the United States.

Comments on the UNFCCC Treaty

The UNFCCC treaty is shown in its entirety in Appendix 5.

It is not possible to revise or amend the treaty. We must *exit* it entirely.

Summary of UNFCCC treaty

Some passages have been italicized in the text of the treaty in Appendix 5. The following comments refer to those italicized passages.

[I]   Establishes that CO2 emissions of developing countries will increase.

[II]   Creates an opening for other countries to sue the United States because its emissions cross into other countries.

[III]   Incorporates the concept of "common but differentiated responsibilities and respective capabilities." This concept is used to justify requiring developed countries, such as the United States, to bear the bulk of the financial and other burdens in efforts to cut CO2 emissions.

[IV]   Incorporates the precautionary principle that precludes adopting new technologies unless they can be guaranteed not to cause any harm. It is a controversial concept because it essentially stops development. Electricity, for example, if it had been subject to the precautionary principle, might never have been allowed to be developed.

[V]   Requires the adoption of programs to cut CO2 and other greenhouse gas emissions. This is a useless and expensive endeavor since, as established in the previous chapters, cutting CO2 and other greenhouse gas emissions cannot stop any adverse effects

32

Comments on the UNFCCC Treaty

on the climate. The United States should not be required to adopt measures that will harm Americans, and which, in fact, will harm peoples around the world.

[VI] Requires American corporations to transfer technology and confidential information without compensation to developing countries. China is a developing country under this treaty.

[VII] While seemingly innocuous, this provision is being used to propagandize global warming and climate change.

CO2 is being promoted, under the guise of education, as the cause of global warming, without any semblance of objectivity concerning the probable effect the sun has on the earth.

[VIII] Requires the United States to needlessly reduce its CO2 emissions. **This paragraph of the UNFCCC treaty could be construed to already obligate the United States to comply with any agreement or protocol under the UNFCCC treaty. Currently, there is a debate as to whether the United States is obligated to comply with the COP 21 Paris accord even if it is not ratified by the U.S. Senate.**

Withdrawing from the UNFCCC treaty would eliminate any possible future misunderstanding with respect to whether the United States is obligated to cut its CO2 and greenhouse gas emissions.

Comments on the UNFCCC Treaty

[IX]   While there might be some scientific value in collecting these data, the United States should not be legally obligated to provide the data to some international body.

[X]   This is the paragraph that has given rise to the United States having to give taxpayer dollars to a development fund. The United States should not be obligated to give taxpayer dollars to other countries, especially when it's for a useless purpose. The Green Climate Fund is to be $100 billion per year by 2020.

    The United States has pledged to give $3 billion taxpayer dollars to the fund. The Obama administration gave $500 million to the Green Climate Fund in 2016.

[XI]   Use of UNFCCC to propagandize climate change.

[XII]   Establishes the bureaucracy for implementing CO_2 emissions. It pays for the 10,000 or so people attending COP meetings every year, a huge waste of money that could be better used to build infrastructure that would actually help people improve their lives.

[XIII]   A means to perpetuate the bureaucracy.

[XIV]   Establishes that COP meetings will be held every year, at great cost, whether needed or not.

[XV]   Allows any non-governmental organization to attend COP meetings. Typically these have been organizations that have been strongly in favor of adopting regulations for cutting CO_2 emissions.

[XVI]   Redundant, in that countries have scientific organizations, such as National Oceanic and Atmospheric Administration, that can do this work, if necessary. Merely adds to the bureaucracy.

[XVII] Unnecessary bureaucracy.

[XVIII] Article 12 of the UNFCCC treaty details the requirements called for in previous articles. For example, this section requires the submission of information that is difficult and costly to gather.

Article 12 of the treaty also establishes where developing countries can propose projects that will be paid for by developed countries.

[XIX] The United States is placed in the position of having any disagreement arising from the UNFCCC treaty judged either by a conciliatory committee composed of other member countries or by the International Court. The United States would always be subject to having countries hostile to the United States, such as Iran, judging the actions of the United States.

[XX] Amendments to the treaty can be made by a vote of 3/4th of the member countries where the United States has one vote. While the United States would not have to accept any amendment, the United States would be placed in the position of being at odds with other countries and open to continual criticism.

[XXI] The United States has one vote among the 197 members. Many of the members countries, such as Iran, are hostile to the interests of the United States. They can vote against the interests of the United States and the United States has few options for overturning the vote.

Comments on the UNFCCC Treaty

[XXII] Any country can withdraw from the treaty by providing written notification of its withdrawal, which would go into effect one year after being submitted.

Withdrawal releases the country from all agreements and protocols made under the UNFCCC treaty.

Appendix 1

Carbon Capture and Sequestration

Carbon capture and sequestration (CCS) has been promoted as the only method by which CO_2 emissions can be kept from entering the atmosphere from existing power plants and industrial processes so that atmospheric CO_2 can be kept below 450 ppm and temperature increases can be kept below 2 degrees C.[20]

There are two fundamental problems with CCS that make the concept unworkable:

First, there is the problem of capturing CO_2.

Second, there is the problem of sequestering CO_2 underground with absolute certainty it will never escape to the atmosphere for thousands of years.

The initial hurdle is to develop methods for capturing CO_2 from existing power plants. Several methods have been proposed and tried.

The main problem with carbon capture from existing power plants is that the process for capturing and compressing CO_2 requires electricity. A 300 MW power plant would have to use 30 to 40 percent of the electricity it generates to capture and compress the CO_2 it produced. That means the plant would be able to produce only 200 MW of electricity for the grid.

Carbon capture in traditional coal-fired and natural gas power plants would require building many more new power plants to replace the electricity lost from capturing and compressing the CO_2 so that it could be transported by pipeline to where it could be injected underground.

Carbon Capture and Sequestration

Another recently proposed method is to use the exhaust stream from a coal-fired or natural gas power plant in a fuel cell which concentrates the CO_2, thereby making the capture process easier.

The fuel cell also generates electricity that can help reduce or offset the use of electricity from the power plant, where such extraneous use is referred to as a parasitic loss. The process is still experimental, and there is no answer yet as to how much the parasitic losses can be reduced.

While the fuel cell sounds appealing, it actually is a more expensive alternative to constructing new coal-fired or natural gas power plants for replacing parasitic losses. It accomplishes this instead, by adding an expensive fuel cell generating capability to an existing power plant. In short, it doesn't eliminate the need to build replacement power.

Another method for capturing CO_2 is to build integrated gasification combined cycle (IGCC) power plants.

IGCC power plants essentially cook the coal to create a synthetic gas (syngas) composed mostly of CO_2 and hydrogen. The CO_2 is extracted from the syngas and the remaining gases, mostly hydrogen, are burned in a gas turbine to generate electricity.

Three IGCC plants have been built in the United States, each at a cost of nearly $6,000/KW, which is about what a new nuclear power plant costs.

Once the CO_2 has been captured, it must be compressed to around 2,000 psi and transported to where it can be injected into a geologic formation underground.

Carbon Capture and Sequestration

The Pacific Northwest National Laboratory has estimated it would require building around 20,000 miles of new pipelines in the United States to transport the CO_2.[21]

Europe has also established that a pipeline network of several thousand miles would be required for transporting liquid CO_2 to where it can be sequestered.[22]

Some people point to the fact that small quantities of CO_2 have been used for enhanced oil recovery (EOR), and that a few pipelines have been built for this purpose. But the quantities involved have been tiny compared to what would be required if sequestration were to be relied on to dispose of CO_2 around the world.

Statoil has captured CO_2 from its production of natural gas at the Sleipner field off the coast of Norway. Starting in 1996, Statoil captured around 1 million tons of CO_2 annually, sequestering it in a nearby geologic formation.

As a result, Statoil has captured and sequestered approximately 20 million tons of CO_2.

The 20 million tons captured by Statoil over two decades is minuscule compared with the approximately 2,000 million metric tons (MMT) produced *every year* just from the generation of electricity in the United States.

There have been a few other examples of sequestration, with Algeria and Canada being the two most prominent. But these quantities have also been small compared with what would have to be sequestered if CCS were to be the means for preventing atmospheric CO_2 from reaching levels above 450 ppm.

Carbon Capture and Sequestration

Most critical for CCS to be successful is that there must be a guarantee that the millions and millions of tons of sequestered CO_2 won't leak into the atmosphere over the next several thousand years.

No one can guarantee that CO_2 won't leak back into the atmosphere, especially since there have been examples of gases, supposedly secured in underground storage, leaking into the atmosphere.

There have been at least three examples of natural gas that was supposedly stored safely underground leaking into the atmosphere.

- Most recently, there was the Aliso Canyon leak in California on October 23, 2015.

- A leak through a system of unknown salt wells and piping caused an explosion in Hutchison, Kansas in 2011, which resulted in extensive damage and the deaths two people.

- A storage facility in Liberty County, Texas, 16 miles north of Houston, had a well control incident and natural gas fire that took over six days to extinguish.

These three examples demonstrate that sequestered CO_2 can, and probably will, leak back into the atmosphere.

The costs associated with carbon capture, the need to build many new power plants to replace electricity lost from the capture process, or the need to build many new IGCC power plants at an exorbitant cost, all make CCS unrealistic.

The fact that sequestered CO_2 will probably leak back into the atmosphere means that CCS cannot be relied on to keep CO_2 out of the atmosphere. In summary, CCS is an unworkable concept.

Appendix 2

Alternative Uses of CO2

There is a steady stream of proposals for converting CO_2 into products that would remove CO_2 from the atmosphere. These are typically based on laboratory experiments, with little prospect for commercial or practical development.

Two of the latest are:

- Converting CO_2 into ethanol
- Converting CO_2 into gasoline

Converting CO2 into ethanol

A recent press release from DOE's Oak Ridge National Laboratory created a media stir, with reporting such as:

> The [CO2 to ethanol] process could be used to store excess electricity generated [by] wind and solar. ... It could help balance a grid supplied by intermittent renewable sources.[23]

Unfortunately, two factors relegate this discovery to the category of wishful thinking.

First, there is the scientific fact that the process requires more energy to produce ethanol from CO_2 than is released when the ethanol is burned. The energy input is greater than the energy output.

We have not yet discovered perpetual motion. Electricity is required to produce ethanol from CO_2, and the process has a yield of only 63%.

Alternative Uses of CO2

Electricity produced from wind during the day will almost certainly be used on the grid. There may be some small amount of electricity produced by wind at night that could be used to produce ethanol, but the quantities would not be meaningful.[24]

Finally, the scientific paper describing the process admits:

> The process probably precludes economic viability for this catalyst. And,

> The entire reaction mechanism has not yet been elucidated.

The media created the impression that a process was accidentally discovered that could remove CO_2 from the atmosphere and halt climate change while also mitigating the intermittent problems associated with wind and solar, but both propositions are false.

Converting CO2 into gasoline

MIT announced a new catalyst that could help transform CO_2 into gasoline.

MIT also announced, "The initial demonstration is just at a small laboratory scale, and ... much work remains for this to become a practical approach to manufacturing transportation fuels."[25]

In both instances, the CO_2 still needs to be captured from the flue gases of coal-fired and natural gas power plants, which, as described earlier, requires the derating of the power plants by 30% with the accompanying need to build new power plants to replace the lost capacity.

Alternative Uses of CO2

Nothing is on the horizon to convert CO_2 to some other product that would affect how to dispose of captured CO_2 between now and 2050.

Until a process has been developed that is proven to be able to convert CO_2 to another product or form outside the laboratory and to scale, it's prudent to proceed on the basis that such a process remains a pleasant fantasy.

Appendix 3

Storage

Pumped storage and compressed air energy storage (CAES) can store large amounts of electricity, but there are insufficient locations around the United States to accommodate the approximately 400,000 MW of storage needed.

Only two CAES facilities have been built thus far: one at Huntorf, Germany, in 1978, and the second at McIntosh, Alabama, in 1991. Huntorf is rated 321 MW, while McIntosh is rated 110 MW. A third CAES facility, to be rated around 300 MW, is proposed for the Intermountain Power Generation site in Utah.

Note that these amounts of storage using CAES are minuscule when compared with the amount of storage needed.

Pumped storage was reportedly first used in the United States by Connecticut Light and Power in 1927, to pump water, using electricity generated by the hydropower plant, back to the lake that was the source of water for the hydropower plant.

Pumped storage, a proven method for storing electricity, is frequently opposed by various groups for environmental reasons,[26] making pumped storage an unusable alternative in many locations.

Currently there is 20,000 MW of pumped storage in the United States, with the suggested potential for an additional 31,000 MW, primarily in the West.[27] While substantial, it still falls far short of the storage capacity needed for eliminating a large portion of fossil fuel generating capacity.

Storage

Salt pits at concentrating solar power (CSP) plants are a form of thermal storage. Salt was used for storage at the Crescent Dunes CSP plant near Tonopah, Nevada, in 2016, which extended the plant's ability to generate electricity for around ten hours at night.

Using ice in cooling systems is another method of thermal storage.

Batteries and other possible storage media lack the necessary size and have other limitations. Batteries, for example, have relatively short lives and would have to be replaced periodically, which adds to their cost as a storage option.

Storage, using batteries, costs at least $2,000,000 per MW. A recent trial by Pacific Gas & Electric of battery storage cost more than twice this amount.[28]

Pumped storage and CAES can cost even more. These costs would vastly increase the investment required for using wind or solar.

Appendix 4

Decline of Nuclear Power in the United States

The United States currently has approximately 100 nuclear power plants in operation. Four new nuclear plants are under construction: two in Georgia and two in South Carolina.

These 104 plants will continue to produce about 20% of U.S. electricity ... for a few more years, and then the decline begins.

When first built and approved, nuclear power plants are given a 40-year operating license. To continue operating after 40 years, they are required by law to get a 20-year license renewal.

Approximately 87 of the 100 existing plants have received their 20-year license renewals, and it has been widely assumed the remaining units will also receive renewals, though a few are now in question due to environmental agitation.

Importantly, all existing nuclear power plants will have to obtain a second 20-year renewal when the initial 20-year renewal expires.

The first of the units that obtained their initial 20 year renewal will need to obtain their second 20-year renewal in the mid-2030s, about 20 years from now.

While obtaining the first 20-year renewal was reasonable, a second 20-year renewal may be problematic. At the end of a second 20-year renewal these nuclear power plants will be 80 years old, and it's logical to believe that these plants will be wearing out.

Decline of Nuclear Power in the United States

Nothing lasts forever, and everything from embrittlement of the reactor containment vessel to aging piping, valves and control systems could be cause for concern. There is every reason to believe that most of these plants will not receive a second 20-year license renewal.

Without a second 20-year renewal, existing nuclear power plants will have to begin shutting down in the mid-2030s.

Unless new nuclear power plants are built, the amount of electricity supplied from nuclear power plants in the United States will begin to rapidly decline.

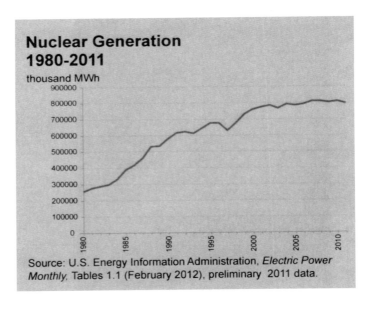

Source: U.S. Energy Information Administration, *Electric Power Monthly*, Tables 1.1 (February 2012), preliminary 2011 data.

Figure 3 from EIA

Decline of Nuclear Power in the United States

The cost of new nuclear plants has grown to a staggering $6,000/KW.

With low natural gas prices, and the possibility that new ultra-supercritical coal-fired power plants[29] can be built at less than half the cost of nuclear power plants, the economics mitigate against building new nuclear plants in the United States.

With proposals for Yucca Mountain storage of spent nuclear fuel stalled in political battles, and with the public emotionally opposed to nuclear power, it would seem that nuclear will be in terminal decline in the United States.

There's a very strong possibility that nuclear will supply less than 5% of our electricity by 2100.

Even small modular nuclear power plants cost $6,000 / KW, so they may also be too expensive when compared with alternatives.

Meanwhile, the situation elsewhere in the world is different.

A total of 64,000 MW of nuclear power plant capacity is being built elsewhere in the world, which translates into approximately 64 new nuclear power plants if their average size is 1,000 MW.

It's possible the Trump administration will revive Yucca Mountain for storage, as it is essential for storing the spent fuel rods already in existence. Whether nuclear power can be revived is another issue.

Appendix 5

Text of UNFCCC Treaty

(The bold Roman numerals in brackets identify comments made in Chapter 5, and are not part of the treaty.)

UNITED NATIONS FRAMEWORK CONVENTION ON
CLIMATE CHANGE

UNITED NATIONS 1992

The Parties to this Convention,

Acknowledging that change in the Earth's climate and its adverse effects are a common concern of humankind,

Concerned that human activities have been substantially increasing the atmospheric concentrations of greenhouse gases, that these increases enhance the natural greenhouse effect, and that this will result on average in an additional warming of the Earth's surface and atmosphere and may adversely affect natural ecosystems and humankind,

[I] *Noting that the largest share of historical and current global emissions of greenhouse gases has originated in developed countries, that per capita emissions in developing countries are still relatively low and that the share of global emissions originating in developing countries will grow to meet their social and development needs,*

Aware of the role and importance in terrestrial and marine ecosystems of sinks and reservoirs of greenhouse gases,

Text of UNFCCC Treaty

Noting that there are many uncertainties in predictions of climate change, particularly with regard to the timing, magnitude and regional patterns thereof,

Acknowledging that the global nature of climate change calls for the widest possible cooperation by all countries and their participation in an effective and appropriate international response, in accordance with their common but differentiated responsibilities and respective capabilities and their social and economic conditions,

Recalling the pertinent provisions of the Declaration of the United Nations Conference on the Human Environment, adopted at Stockholm on 16 June 1972,

[II] Recalling also that States have, in accordance with the Charter of the United Nations and the principles of international law, the sovereign right to exploit their own resources pursuant to their own environmental and developmental policies, and the responsibility to *ensure that activities within their jurisdiction or control do not cause damage to the environment of other States or of areas beyond the limits of national jurisdiction,*

Reaffirming the principle of sovereignty of States in international cooperation to address climate change,

Recognizing that States should enact effective environmental legislation, that environmental standards, management objectives and priorities should reflect the environmental and developmental context to which they apply, and that standards applied by some countries may be inappropriate and of unwarranted economic and social cost to other countries, in particular developing countries,

Text of UNFCCC Treaty

<u>Recalling</u> the provisions of General Assembly resolution 44/228 of 22 December 1989 on the United Nations Conference on Environment and Development, and resolutions 43/53 of 6 December 1988, 44/207 of 22 December 1989, 45/212 of 21 December 1990 and 46/169 of 19 December 1991 on protection of global climate for present and future generations of mankind,

<u>Recalling</u> also the provisions of General Assembly resolution 44/206 of 22 December 1989 on the possible adverse effects of sea-level rise on islands and coastal areas, particularly low-lying coastal areas and the pertinent provisions of General Assembly resolution 44/172 of 19 December 1989 on the implementation of the Plan of Action to Combat Desertification,

<u>Recalling</u> further the Vienna Convention for the Protection of the Ozone Layer, 1985, and the Montreal Protocol on Substances that Deplete the Ozone Layer, 1987, as adjusted and amended on 29 June 1990,

<u>Noting</u> the Ministerial Declaration of the Second World Climate Conference adopted on 7 November 1990,

<u>Conscious</u> of the valuable analytical work being conducted by many States on climate change and of the important contributions of the World Meteorological Organization, the United Nations Environment Programme and other organs, organizations and bodies of the United Nations system, as well as other international and intergovernmental bodies, to the exchange of results of scientific research and the coordination of research,

<u>Recognizing</u> that steps required to understand and address climate change will be environmentally, socially and economically most effective if they are based on relevant scientific, technical and

economic considerations and continually re-evaluated in the light of new findings in these areas,

Recognizing that various actions to address climate change can be justified economically in their own right and can also help in solving other environmental problems,

Recognizing also the need for developed countries to take immediate action in a flexible manner on the basis of clear priorities, as a first step towards comprehensive response strategies at the global, national and, where agreed, regional levels that take into account all greenhouse gases, with due consideration of their relative contributions to the enhancement of the greenhouse effect,

Recognizing further that low-lying and other small island countries, countries with low-lying coastal, arid and semi-arid areas or areas liable to floods, drought and desertification, and developing countries with fragile mountainous ecosystems are particularly vulnerable to the adverse effects of climate change,

Recognizing the special difficulties of those countries, especially developing countries, whose economies are particularly dependent on fossil fuel production, use and exportation, as a consequence of action taken on limiting greenhouse gas emissions,

Affirming that responses to climate change should be coordinated with social and economic development in an integrated manner with a view to avoiding adverse impacts on the latter, taking into full account the legitimate priority needs of developing countries for the achievement of sustained economic growth and the eradication of poverty,

Text of UNFCCC Treaty

Recognizing that all countries, especially developing countries, need access to resources required to achieve sustainable social and economic development and that, in order for developing countries to progress towards that goal, their energy consumption will need to grow taking into account the possibilities for achieving greater energy efficiency and for controlling greenhouse gas emissions in general, including through the application of new technologies on terms which make such an application economically and socially beneficial,

Determined to protect the climate system for present and future generations,

Have agreed as follows:

ARTICLE 1 — DEFINITIONS

For the purposes of this Convention:

1. "Adverse effects of climate change" means changes in the physical environment or biota resulting from climate change which have significant deleterious effects on the composition, resilience or productivity of natural and managed ecosystems or on the operation of socio-economic systems or on human health and welfare.

2. "Climate change" means a change of climate which is attributed directly or indirectly to human activity that alters the composition of the global atmosphere and which is in addition to natural climate variability observed over comparable time periods.

Text of UNFCCC Treaty

3. "Climate system" means the totality of the atmosphere, hydrosphere, biosphere and geosphere and their interactions.

4. "Emissions" means the release of greenhouse gases and/or their precursors into the atmosphere over a specified area and period of time.

5. "Greenhouse gases" means those gaseous constituents of the atmosphere, both natural and anthropogenic, that absorb and re-emit infrared radiation.

6. "Regional economic integration organization" means an organization constituted by sovereign States of a given region which has competence in respect of matters governed by this Convention or its protocols and has been duly authorized, in accordance with its internal procedures, to sign, ratify, accept, approve or accede to the instruments concerned.

7. "Reservoir" means a component or components of the climate system where a greenhouse gas or a precursor of a greenhouse gas is stored.

8. "Sink" means any process, activity or mechanism which removes a greenhouse gas, an aerosol or a precursor of a greenhouse gas from the atmosphere.

9. "Source" means any process or activity which releases a greenhouse gas, an aerosol or a precursor of a greenhouse gas into the atmosphere.

Text of UNFCCC Treaty

ARTICLE 2 — OBJECTIVE

The ultimate objective of this Convention and any related legal instruments that the Conference of the Parties may adopt is to achieve, in accordance with the relevant provisions of the Convention, stabilization of greenhouse gas concentrations in the atmosphere at a level that would prevent dangerous anthropogenic interference with the climate system. Such a level should be achieved within a time-frame sufficient to allow ecosystems to adapt naturally to climate change, to ensure that food production is not threatened and to enable economic development to proceed in a sustainable manner.

ARTICLE 3 — PRINCIPLES

In their actions to achieve the objective of the Convention and to implement its provisions, the Parties shall be guided, inter alia, by the following:

[III] 1. The Parties should protect the climate system for the benefit of present and future generations of humankind, on the basis of equity and *in accordance with their common but differentiated responsibilities and respective capabilities. Accordingly, the developed country Parties should take the lead in combating climate change and the adverse effects thereof.*

2. The specific needs and special circumstances of developing country Parties, especially those that are particularly vulnerable to the adverse effects of climate change, and of those Parties, especially developing country Parties, that would have to bear

a disproportionate or abnormal burden under the Convention, should be given full consideration.

[IV] 3. *The Parties should take precautionary measures to anticipate, prevent or minimize the causes of climate change and mitigate its adverse effects.* Where there are threats of serious or irreversible damage, lack of full scientific certainty should not be used as a reason for postponing such measures, taking into account that policies and measures to deal with climate change should be cost-effective so as to ensure global benefits at the lowest possible cost. To achieve this, such policies and measures should take into account different socio-economic contexts, be comprehensive, cover all relevant sources, sinks and reservoirs of greenhouse gases and adaptation, and comprise all economic sectors. Efforts to address climate change may be carried out cooperatively by interested Parties.

4. The Parties have a right to, and should, promote sustainable development. Policies and measures to protect the climate system against human-induced change should be appropriate for the specific conditions of each Party and should be integrated with national development programmes, taking into account that economic development is essential for adopting measures to address climate change.

5. The Parties should cooperate to promote a supportive and open international economic system that would lead to sustainable economic growth and development in all Parties, particularly developing country Parties, thus enabling them better to address the problems of climate change. Measures taken to combat climate change, including unilateral ones, should not

constitute a means of arbitrary or unjustifiable discrimination or a disguised restriction on international trade.

ARTICLE 4 — COMMITMENTS

1. All Parties, taking into account their common but differentiated responsibilities and their specific national and regional development priorities, objectives and circumstances, shall:

   (a) Develop, periodically update, publish and make available to the Conference of the Parties, in accordance with Article 12, national inventories of anthropogenic emissions by sources and removals by sinks of all greenhouse gases not controlled by the Montreal Protocol, using comparable methodologies to be agreed upon by the Conference of the Parties;

   [V] (b) Formulate, implement, publish and regularly update national and, where appropriate, regional programmes containing measures to mitigate *climate change by addressing anthropogenic emissions by sources and removals by sinks of all greenhouse gases not controlled by the Montreal Protocol, and measures to facilitate adequate adaptation to climate change;*

   [VI] (c) *Promote and cooperate in the development, application and diffusion, including transfer, of technologies, practices and processes that control, reduce or prevent anthropogenic emissions of greenhouse gases not controlled by the Montreal Protocol in all relevant sectors, including the energy, transport, industry, agriculture, forestry and waste management sectors;*

(d) Promote sustainable management, and promote and cooperate in the conservation and enhancement, as appropriate, of sinks and reservoirs of all greenhouse gases not controlled by the Montreal Protocol, including biomass, forests and oceans as well as other terrestrial, coastal and marine ecosystems;

(e) Cooperate in preparing for adaptation to the impacts of climate change; develop and elaborate appropriate and integrated plans for coastal zone management, water resources and agriculture, and for the protection and rehabilitation of areas, particularly in Africa, affected by drought and desertification, as well as floods;

(f) Take climate change considerations into account, to the extent feasible, in their relevant social, economic and environmental policies and actions, and employ appropriate methods, for example impact assessments, formulated and determined nationally, with a view to minimizing adverse effects on the economy, on public health and on the quality of the environment, of projects or measures undertaken by them to mitigate or adapt to climate change;

(g) Promote and cooperate in scientific, technological, technical, socio-economic and other research, systematic observation and development of data archives related to the climate system and intended to further the understanding and to reduce or eliminate the remaining uncertainties regarding the causes, effects, magnitude and timing of climate change and the economic and social consequences of various response strategies;

Text of UNFCCC Treaty

(h) Promote and cooperate in the full, open and prompt exchange of relevant scientific, technological, technical, socio-economic and legal information related to the climate system and climate change, and to the economic and social consequences of various response strategies;

[VII] (i) *Promote and cooperate in education, training and public awareness related to climate change and encourage the widest participation in this process, including that of non-governmental organizations; and*

(j) Communicate to the Conference of the Parties information related to implementation, in accordance with Article 12.

2. The developed country Parties and other Parties included in Annex I commit themselves specifically as provided for in the following:

[VIII] (a) *Each of these Parties shall adopt national policies and take corresponding measures on the mitigation of climate change, by limiting its anthropogenic emissions of greenhouse gases and protecting and enhancing its greenhouse gas sinks and reservoirs.* These policies and measures will demonstrate that developed countries are taking the lead in modifying longer-term trends in anthropogenic emissions consistent with the objective of the Convention, recognizing that the return by the end of the present decade to earlier levels of anthropogenic emissions of carbon dioxide and other greenhouse gases not controlled by the Montreal Protocol would contribute to such modification, and taking into account the differences in these Parties' starting points and approaches, economic structures and resource bases, the need to maintain strong and sustainable economic growth, available technologies and other individual circumstances, as well as the need for equitable and appropriate contributions by each of these Parties to the global effort regarding that objective. These Parties may implement such policies and measures jointly with other Parties and may assist other Parties in contributing to the achievement of the objective of the Convention and, in particular, that of this subparagraph;

(1) This includes policies and measures adopted by regional economic integration organizations.

[IX] (b) In order to promote progress to this end, each of these Parties shall communicate, within six months of the entry into force of the Convention for it and *periodically thereafter, and in accordance with Article 12, detailed information on its policies and measures referred to in subparagraph (a) above, as well as on its resulting projected anthropogenic emissions by sources and removals by sinks of greenhouse gases* not controlled by the Montreal Protocol for the period referred to in subparagraph (a), with the aim of returning individually or jointly to their 1990 levels these anthropogenic emissions of carbon dioxide and other greenhouse gases not controlled by the Montreal Protocol. This information will be reviewed by the Conference of the Parties, at its first session and periodically thereafter, in accordance with Article 7;

(c) Calculations of emissions by sources and removals by sinks of greenhouse gases for the purposes of subparagraph (b) above should take into account the best available scientific knowledge, including of the effective capacity of sinks and the respective contributions of such gases to climate change. The Conference of the Parties shall consider and agree on methodologies for these calculations at its first session and review them regularly thereafter;

(d) The Conference of the Parties shall, at its first session, review the adequacy of subparagraphs (a) and (b) above. Such review shall be carried out in the light of the best available scientific information and assessment on climate change and its impacts, as well as relevant technical, social and economic information. Based on this review, the Conference of the Parties shall take appropriate action, which may include the adoption of amendments to the commitments in subparagraphs (a) and (b) above. The Conference of the Parties, at its first session, shall also take decisions regarding criteria for joint implementation as indicated in subparagraph (a) above. A second review of subparagraphs (a) and (b) shall take place not later than 31 December 1998, and thereafter at regular intervals determined by the Conference of the Parties, until the objective of the Convention is met;

(e) Each of these Parties shall:

   (i) Coordinate as appropriate with other such Parties, relevant economic and administrative instruments developed to achieve the objective of the Convention; and

   (ii) Identify and periodically review its own policies and practices which encourage activities that lead to greater levels of anthropogenic emissions of greenhouse gases not controlled by the Montreal Protocol than would otherwise occur;

(f) The Conference of the Parties shall review, no later than 31 December 1998, available information with a view to taking decisions regarding such amendments to the lists in Annexes I and II as may be appropriate, with the approval of the Party concerned;

(g) Any Party not included in Annex I may, in its instrument of ratification, acceptance, approval or accession, or at any time thereafter, notify the Depositary that it intends to be bound by subparagraphs (a) and (b) above. The Depositary shall inform the other signatories and Parties of any such notification.

[X] 3. *The developed country Parties and other developed Parties included in Annex II shall provide new and additional financial resources to meet the agreed full costs incurred by developing country Parties in complying with their obligations under Article 12, paragraph 1. They shall also provide such financial resources, including for the transfer of technology, needed by the developing country Parties to meet the agreed full incremental costs of implementing measures that are covered by paragraph 1 of this Article and that are agreed between a developing country Party and the international entity or entities referred to in Article 11, in accordance with that Article.* The implementation of these commitments shall take into account the need for adequacy and predictability in the flow of funds and the importance of appropriate burden sharing among the developed country Parties.

4. The developed country Parties and other developed Parties included in Annex II shall also assist the developing country Parties that are particularly vulnerable to the adverse effects of climate change in meeting costs of adaptation to those adverse effects.

5. The developed country Parties and other developed Parties included in Annex II shall take all practicable steps to promote, facilitate and finance, as appropriate, the transfer of, or access to, environmentally sound technologies and know-how to other Parties, particularly developing country Parties, to enable them to implement the provisions of the Convention. In this process, the developed country Parties shall support the development and enhancement of endogenous capacities and technologies of developing country Parties. Other Parties and organizations in a position to do so may also assist in facilitating the transfer of such technologies.

6. In the implementation of their commitments under paragraph 2 above, a certain degree of flexibility shall be allowed by the Conference of the Parties to the Parties included in Annex I undergoing the process of transition to a market economy, in order to enhance the ability of these Parties to address climate change, including with regard to the historical level of anthropogenic emissions of greenhouse gases not controlled by the Montreal Protocol chosen as a reference.

7. The extent to which developing country Parties will effectively implement their commitments under the Convention will depend on the effective implementation by developed country Parties of their commitments under the Convention related to financial resources and transfer of technology and will take

fully into account that economic and social development and poverty eradication are the first and overriding priorities of the developing country Parties.

8. In the implementation of the commitments in this Article, the Parties shall give full consideration to what actions are necessary under the Convention, including actions related to funding, insurance and the transfer of technology, to meet the specific needs and concerns of developing country Parties arising from the adverse effects of climate change and/or the impact of the implementation of response measures, especially on:

    (a) Small island countries;
    (b) Countries with low-lying coastal areas;
    (c) Countries with arid and semi-arid areas, forested areas and areas liable to forest decay;
    (d) Countries with areas prone to natural disasters;
    (e) Countries with areas liable to drought and desertification;
    (f) Countries with areas of high urban atmospheric pollution;
    (g) Countries with areas with fragile ecosystems, including mountainous ecosystems;
    (h) Countries whose economies are highly dependent on income generated from the production, processing and export, and/or on consumption of fossil fuels and associated energy-intensive products; and
    (i) Land-locked and transit countries.

    Further, the Conference of the Parties may take actions, as appropriate, with respect to this paragraph.

9. The Parties shall take full account of the specific needs and special situations of the least developed countries in their actions with regard to funding and transfer of technology.

10. The Parties shall, in accordance with Article 10, take into consideration in the implementation of the commitments of the Convention the situation of Parties, particularly developing country Parties, with economies that are vulnerable to the adverse effects of the implementation of measures to respond to climate change. This applies notably to Parties with economies that are highly dependent on income generated from the production, processing and export, and/or consumption of fossil fuels and associated energy-intensive products and/or the use of fossil fuels for which such Parties have serious difficulties in switching to alternatives.

ARTICLE 5 — RESEARCH AND SYSTEMATIC OBSERVATION

In carrying out their commitments under Article 4, paragraph 1(g), the Parties shall:

(a) Support and further develop, as appropriate, international and intergovernmental programmes and networks or organizations aimed at defining, conducting, assessing and financing research, data collection and systematic observation, taking into account the need to minimize duplication of effort;

(b) Support international and intergovernmental efforts to strengthen systematic observation and national scientific and technical research capacities and capabilities, particularly in developing countries, and to promote access to, and the exchange of, data and analyses thereof obtained from areas beyond national jurisdiction; and

(c) Take into account the particular concerns and needs of developing countries and cooperate in improving their endogenous capacities and capabilities to participate in the efforts referred to in subparagraphs (a) and (b) above.

ARTICLE 6 — EDUCATION, TRAINING AND PUBLIC AWARENESS

In carrying out their commitments under Article 4, paragraph 1(i), the Parties shall:

[XI] (a) *Promote and facilitate at the national and, as appropriate, subregional and regional levels, and in accordance with national laws and regulations, and within their respective capacities:*

(i) *The development and implementation of educational and public awareness programmes on climate change and its effects;*

(ii) Public access to information on climate change and its effects;

(iii) Public participation in addressing climate change and its effects and developing adequate responses; and

(iv) Training of scientific, technical and managerial personnel.

(b) Cooperate in and promote, at the international level, and, where appropriate, using existing bodies:

(i) *The development and exchange of educational and public awareness material on climate change and its effects; and*

(ii) *The development and implementation of education and training programmes, including the strengthening of national institutions and the exchange or secondment of personnel to train experts in this field, in particular for developing countries.*

[XII] *ARTICLE 7 — CONFERENCE OF THE PARTIES*

1. A Conference of the Parties is hereby established.

2. The Conference of the Parties, as the supreme body of this Convention, shall keep under regular review the implementation of the Convention and any related legal instruments that the Conference of the Parties may adopt, and shall make, within its mandate, the decisions necessary to promote the effective implementation of the Convention. To this end, it shall:

(a) Periodically examine the obligations of the Parties and the institutional arrangements under the Convention, in the light of the objective of the Convention, the experience gained in its implementation and the evolution of scientific and technological knowledge;

(b) Promote and facilitate the exchange of information on measures adopted by the Parties to address climate change and its effects, taking into account the differing circumstances, responsibilities and capabilities of the

Parties and their respective commitments under the Convention;

(c) Facilitate, at the request of two or more Parties, the coordination of measures adopted by them to address climate change and its effects, taking into account the differing circumstances, responsibilities and capabilities of the Parties and their respective commitments under the Convention;

(d) Promote and guide, in accordance with the objective and provisions of the Convention, the development and periodic refinement of comparable methodologies, to be agreed on by the Conference of the Parties, inter alia, for preparing inventories of greenhouse gas emissions by sources and removals by sinks, and for evaluating the effectiveness of measures to limit the emissions and enhance the removals of these gases;

(e) Assess, on the basis of all information made available to it in accordance with the provisions of the Convention, the implementation of the Convention by the Parties, the overall effects of the measures taken pursuant to the Convention, in particular environmental, economic and social effects as well as their cumulative impacts and the extent to which progress towards the objective of the Convention is being achieved;

(f) Consider and adopt regular reports on the implementation of the Convention and ensure their publication;

(g) Make recommendations on any matters necessary for the implementation of the Convention;

(h) Seek to mobilize financial resources in accordance with Article 4, paragraphs 3, 4 and 5, and Article 11;

[XIII] (i) *Establish such subsidiary bodies as are deemed necessary for the implementation of the Convention;*

(j) Review reports submitted by its subsidiary bodies and provide guidance to them;

(k) Agree upon and adopt, by consensus, rules of procedure and financial rules for itself and for any subsidiary bodies;

(l) Seek and utilize, where appropriate, the services and cooperation of, and information provided by, competent international organizations and intergovernmental and *non-governmental bodies;* and

(m) Exercise such other functions as are required for the achievement of the objective of the Convention as well as all other functions assigned to it under the Convention.

3. The Conference of the Parties shall, at its first session, adopt its own rules of procedure as well as those of the subsidiary bodies established by the Convention, which shall include decision-making procedures for matters not already covered by decision-making procedures stipulated in the Convention. Such procedures may include specified majorities required for the adoption of particular decisions.

[XIV] 4. The first session of the Conference of the Parties shall be convened by the interim secretariat referred to in Article 21 and shall take place not later than one year after the date of entry into force of the Convention. *Thereafter, ordinary sessions of the Conference of the Parties shall be held every year* unless otherwise decided by the Conference of the Parties.

5. Extraordinary sessions of the Conference of the Parties shall be held at such other times as may be deemed necessary by the Conference, or at the written request of any Party, provided that, within six months of the request being communicated to the Parties by the secretariat, it is supported by at least one-third of the Parties.

[XV] 6. The United Nations, its specialized agencies and the International Atomic Energy Agency, as well as any State member thereof or observers thereto not Party to the Convention, may be represented at sessions of the Conference of the Parties as observers. Any body or agency, whether national or international, *governmental or non-governmental,* which is qualified in matters covered by the Convention, and which has informed the secretariat of its wish to be represented at a session of the Conference of the Parties as an observer, may be so admitted unless at least one third of the Parties present object. The admission and participation of observers shall be subject to the rules of procedure adopted by the Conference of the Parties.

ARTICLE 8 — SECRETARIAT

1. A secretariat is hereby established.

2. The functions of the secretariat shall be:

    (a) To make arrangements for sessions of the Conference of the Parties and its subsidiary bodies established under the Convention and to provide them with services as required;

    (b) To compile and transmit reports submitted to it;

(c) To facilitate assistance to the Parties, particularly developing country Parties, on request, in the compilation and communication of information required in accordance with the provisions of the Convention;

(d) To prepare reports on its activities and present them to the Conference of the Parties;

(e) To ensure the necessary coordination with the secretariats of other relevant international bodies;

(f) To enter, under the overall guidance of the Conference of the Parties, into such administrative and contractual arrangements as may be required for the effective discharge of its functions; and

(g) To perform the other secretariat functions specified in the Convention and in any of its protocols and such other functions as may be determined by the Conference of the Parties.

3. The Conference of the Parties, at its first session, shall designate a permanent secretariat and make arrangements for its functioning.

ARTICLE 9 — SUBSIDIARY BODY FOR SCIENTIFIC AND TECHNOLOGICAL ADVICE

[XVI] 1. *A subsidiary body for scientific and technological advice is hereby established to provide the Conference of the Parties and, as appropriate, its other subsidiary bodies with timely information and advice on scientific and technological matters relating to the Convention.* This body shall be open to

73

participation by all Parties and shall be multidisciplinary. It shall comprise government representatives competent in the relevant field of expertise. It shall report regularly to the Conference of the Parties on all aspects of its work.

2. Under the guidance of the Conference of the Parties, and drawing upon existing competent international bodies, this body shall:

   (a) Provide assessments of the state of scientific knowledge relating to climate change and its effects;

   (b) Prepare scientific assessments on the effects of measures taken in the implementation of the Convention;

   (c) Identify innovative, efficient and state-of-the-art technologies and know-how and advise on the ways and means of promoting development and/or transferring such technologies;

   (d) Provide advice on scientific programmes, international cooperation in research and development related to climate change, as well as on ways and means of supporting endogenous capacity-building in developing countries; and

   (e) Respond to scientific, technological and methodological questions that the Conference of the Parties and its subsidiary bodies may put to the body.

3. The functions and terms of reference of this body may be further elaborated by the Conference of the Parties.

ARTICLE 10 — SUBSIDIARY BODY FOR IMPLEMENTATION

[XVII] 1. *A subsidiary body for implementation is hereby established to assist the Conference of the Parties in the assessment and review of the effective implementation of the Convention.* This body shall be open to participation by all Parties and comprise government representatives who are experts on matters related to climate change. It shall report regularly to the Conference of the Parties on all aspects of its work.

2. Under the guidance of the Conference of the Parties, this body shall:

   (a) Consider the information communicated in accordance with Article 12, paragraph 1, to assess the overall aggregated effect of the steps taken by the Parties in the light of the latest scientific assessments concerning climate change;

   (b) Consider the information communicated in accordance with Article 12, paragraph 2, in order to assist the Conference of the Parties in carrying out the reviews required by Article 4, paragraph 2(d); and

   (c) Assist the Conference of the Parties, as appropriate, in the preparation and implementation of its decisions.

ARTICLE 11 — FINANCIAL MECHANISM

1. A mechanism for the provision of financial resources on a grant or concessional basis, including for the transfer of technology,

is hereby defined. It shall function under the guidance of and be accountable to the Conference of the Parties, which shall decide on its policies, programme priorities and eligibility criteria related to this Convention. Its operation shall be entrusted to one or more existing international entities.

2. The financial mechanism shall have an equitable and balanced representation of all Parties within a transparent system of governance.

3. The Conference of the Parties and the entity or entities entrusted with the operation of the financial mechanism shall agree upon arrangements to give effect to the above paragraphs, which shall include the following:

   (a) Modalities to ensure that the funded projects to address climate change are in conformity with the policies, programme priorities and eligibility criteria established by the Conference of the Parties;

   (b) Modalities by which a particular funding decision may be reconsidered in light of these policies, programme priorities and eligibility criteria;

   (c) Provision by the entity or entities of regular reports to the Conference of the Parties on its funding operations, which is consistent with the requirement for accountability set out in paragraph 1 above; and

   (d) Determination in a predictable and identifiable manner of the amount of funding necessary and available for the implementation of this Convention and the conditions under which that amount shall be periodically reviewed.

4. The Conference of the Parties shall make arrangements to implement the above-mentioned provisions at its first session reviewing and taking into account the interim arrangements referred to in Article 21, paragraph 3, and shall decide whether these interim arrangements shall be maintained. Within four years thereafter, the Conference of the Parties shall review the financial mechanism and take appropriate measures.

5. The developed country Parties may also provide and developing country Parties avail themselves of, financial resources related to the implementation of the Convention through bilateral, regional and other multilateral channels.

ARTICLE 12 — COMMUNICATION OF INFORMATION RELATED TO IMPLEMENTATION

[XVIII] 1. In accordance with Article 4, paragraph 1, each Party shall communicate to the Conference of the Parties, through the secretariat, the following elements of information:

(a) *A national inventory of anthropogenic emissions by sources and removals by sinks of all greenhouse gases not controlled by the Montreal Protocol, to the extent its capacities permit, using comparable methodologies to be promoted and agreed upon by the Conference of the Parties;*

(b) *A general description of steps taken or envisaged by the Party to implement the Convention; and*

(c) Any other information that the Party considers relevant to the achievement of the objective of the Convention and suitable for inclusion in its communication, including, if feasible, material relevant for calculations of global emission trends.

2. Each developed country Party and each other Party included in Annex I shall incorporate in its communication the following elements of information:

    (a) *A detailed description of the policies and measures that it has adopted to implement its commitment under Article 4, paragraphs 2(a) and 2(b); and*

    (b) *A specific estimate of the effects that the policies and measures referred to in subparagraph (a) immediately above will have on anthropogenic emissions by its sources and removals by its sinks of greenhouse gases during the period referred to in Article 4, paragraph 2(a).*

3. In addition, each developed country Party and each other developed Party included in Annex II shall incorporate details of measures taken in accordance with Article 4, paragraphs 3, 4 and 5.

4. Developing country Parties may, on a voluntary basis, *propose projects for financing, including specific technologies, materials, equipment, techniques or practices that would be needed to implement such projects, along with, if possible, an estimate of all incremental costs,* of the reductions of emissions and increments of removals of greenhouse gases, as well as an estimate of the consequent benefits.

5. Each developed country Party and each other Party included in Annex I shall make its initial communication within six months of the entry into force of the Convention for that Party. Each Party not so listed shall make its initial communication within

three years of the entry into force of the Convention for that Party, or of the availability of financial resources in accordance with Article 4, paragraph 3. Parties that are least developed countries may make their initial communication at their discretion. The frequency of subsequent communications by all Parties shall be determined by the Conference of the Parties, taking into account the differentiated timetable set by this paragraph.

6. Information communicated by Parties under this Article shall be transmitted by the secretariat as soon as possible to the Conference of the Parties and to any subsidiary bodies concerned. If necessary, the procedures for the communication of information may be further considered by the Conference of the Parties.

7. From its first session, the Conference of the Parties shall arrange for the provision to developing country Parties of technical and financial support, on request, in compiling and communicating information under this Article, as well as in identifying the technical and financial needs associated with proposed projects and response measures under Article 4. Such support may be provided by other Parties, by competent international organizations and by the secretariat, as appropriate.

8. Any group of Parties may, subject to guidelines adopted by the Conference of the Parties, and to prior notification to the Conference of the Parties, make a joint communication in fulfillment of their obligations under this Article, provided that such a communication includes information on the fulfillment

by each of these Parties of its individual obligations under the Convention.

9. Information received by the secretariat that is designated by a Party as confidential, in accordance with criteria to be established by the Conference of the Parties, shall be aggregated by the secretariat to protect its confidentiality before being made available to any of the bodies involved in the communication and review of information.

10. Subject to paragraph 9 above, and without prejudice to the ability of any Party to make public its communication at any time, the secretariat shall make communications by Parties under this Article publicly available at the time they are submitted to the Conference of the Parties.

ARTICLE 13 — RESOLUTION OF QUESTIONS REGARDING IMPLEMENTATION

The Conference of the Parties shall, at its first session, consider the establishment of a multilateral consultative process, available to Parties on their request, for the resolution of questions regarding the implementation of the Convention.

[XIX] *ARTICLE 14 - SETTLEMENT OF DISPUTES*

1. In the event of a dispute between any two or more Parties concerning the interpretation or application of the Convention, the Parties concerned shall seek a settlement of the dispute through negotiation or any other peaceful means of their own choice.

2. When ratifying, accepting, approving or acceding to the Convention, or at any time thereafter, a Party which is not a regional economic integration organization may declare in a written instrument submitted to the Depositary that, in respect of any dispute concerning the interpretation or application of the Convention, it recognizes as compulsory ipso facto and without special agreement, in relation to any Party accepting the same obligation:

   (a) *Submission of the dispute to the International Court of Justice, and/or*

   (b) *Arbitration in accordance with procedures to be adopted by the Conference of the Parties as soon as practicable, in an annex on arbitration.*

   A Party which is a regional economic integration organization may make a declaration with like effect in relation to arbitration in accordance with the procedures referred to in subparagraph (b) above.

3. A declaration made under paragraph 2 above shall remain in force until it expires in accordance with its terms or until three months after written notice of its revocation has been deposited with the Depositary.

4. A new declaration, a notice of revocation or the expiry of a declaration shall not in any way affect proceedings pending before the International Court of Justice or the arbitral tribunal, unless the parties to the dispute otherwise agree.

5. Subject to the operation of paragraph 2 above, if after twelve months following notification by one Party to another that a dispute exists between them, the Parties concerned have not

been able to settle their dispute through the means mentioned in paragraph 1 above, *the dispute shall be submitted, at the request of any of the parties to the dispute, to conciliation.*

6. *A conciliation commission shall be created upon the request of one of the parties to the dispute. The commission shall be composed of an equal number of members appointed by each party concerned and a chairman chosen jointly by the members appointed by each party.* The commission shall render a recommendatory award, which the parties shall consider in good faith.

7. Additional procedures relating to conciliation shall be adopted by the Conference of the Parties, as soon as practicable, in an annex on conciliation.

8. The provisions of this Article shall apply to any related legal instrument which the Conference of the Parties may adopt, unless the instrument provides otherwise.

ARTICLE 15

[XX] *AMENDMENTS TO THE CONVENTION*

1. Any Party may propose amendments to the Convention.

2. *Amendments to the Convention shall be adopted at an ordinary session of the Conference of the Parties.* The text of any proposed amendment to the Convention shall be communicated to the Parties by the secretariat at least six months before the meeting at which it is proposed for adoption. The secretariat shall also communicate proposed amendments to the

signatories to the Convention and, for information, to the Depositary.

3. The Parties shall make every effort to reach agreement on any proposed amendment to the Convention by consensus. If all efforts at consensus have been exhausted, and no agreement reached, the amendment shall as a last resort be *adopted by a three-fourths majority vote of the Parties present and voting at the meeting*. The adopted amendment shall be communicated by the secretariat to the Depositary, who shall circulate it to all Parties for their acceptance.

4. Instruments of acceptance in respect of an amendment shall be deposited with the Depositary. An amendment adopted in accordance with paragraph 3 above shall enter into force for those Parties having accepted it on the ninetieth day after the date of receipt by the Depositary of an instrument of acceptance by at least three fourths of the Parties to the Convention.

5. The amendment shall enter into force for any other Party on the ninetieth day after the date on which that Party deposits with the Depositary its instrument of acceptance of the said amendment.

6. For the purposes of this Article, "Parties present and voting" means Parties present and casting an affirmative or negative vote.

ARTICLE 16 — ADOPTION AND AMENDMENT OF ANNEXES TO THE CONVENTION

1. Annexes to the Convention shall form an integral part thereof and, unless otherwise expressly provided, a reference to the Convention constitutes at the same time a reference to any annexes thereto. Without prejudice to the provisions of Article 14, paragraphs 2(b) and 7, such annexes shall be restricted to lists, forms and any other material of a descriptive nature that is of a scientific, technical, procedural or administrative character.

2. Annexes to the Convention shall be proposed and adopted in accordance with the procedure set forth in Article 15, paragraphs 2, 3 and 4.

3. An annex that has been adopted in accordance with paragraph 2 above shall enter into force for all Parties to the Convention six months after the date of the communication by the Depositary to such Parties of the adoption of the annex, except for those Parties that have notified the Depositary, in writing, within that period of their non-acceptance of the annex. The annex shall enter into force for Parties which withdraw their notification of non-acceptance on the ninetieth day after the date on which withdrawal of such notification has been received by the Depositary.

4. The proposal, adoption and entry into force of amendments to annexes to the Convention shall be subject to the same procedure as that for the proposal, adoption and entry into force of annexes to the Convention in accordance with paragraphs 2 and 3 above.

5. If the adoption of an annex or an amendment to an annex involves an amendment to the Convention, that annex or

amendment to an annex shall not enter into force until such time as the amendment to the Convention enters into force.

ARTICLE 17 — PROTOCOLS

1. The Conference of the Parties may, at any ordinary session, adopt protocols to the Convention.

2. The text of any proposed protocol shall be communicated to the Parties by the secretariat at least six months before such a session.

3. The requirements for the entry into force of any protocol shall be established by that instrument.

4. Only Parties to the Convention may be Parties to a protocol.

5. Decisions under any protocol shall be taken only by the Parties to the protocol concerned.

ARTICLE 18 — RIGHT TO VOTE

[XXI] 1. *Each Party to the Convention shall have one vote, except as provided for in paragraph 2 below.*

2. Regional economic integration organizations, in matters within their competence, shall exercise their right to vote with a number of votes equal to the number of their member States that are Parties to the Convention. Such an organization shall not exercise its right to vote if any of its member States exercises its right, and vice versa.

Text of UNFCCC Treaty

ARTICLE 19 — DEPOSITARY

The Secretary-General of the United Nations shall be the Depositary of the Convention and of protocols adopted in accordance with Article 17.

ARTICLE 20 — SIGNATURE

This Convention shall be open for signature by States Members of the United Nations or of any of its specialized agencies or that are Parties to the Statute of the International Court of Justice and by regional economic integration organizations at Rio de Janeiro, during the United Nations Conference on Environment and Development, and thereafter at United Nations Headquarters in New York from 20 June 1992 to 19 June 1993.

ARTICLE 21 — INTERIM ARRANGEMENTS

1. The secretariat functions referred to in Article 8 will be carried out on an interim basis by the secretariat established by the General Assembly of the United Nations in its resolution 45/212 of 21 December 1990, until the completion of the first session of the Conference of the Parties.

2. The head of the interim secretariat referred to in paragraph 1 above will cooperate closely with the Intergovernmental Panel on Climate Change to ensure that the Panel can respond to the need for objective scientific and technical advice. Other relevant scientific bodies could also be consulted.

3. The Global Environment Facility of the United Nations Development Programme, the United Nations Environment

Programme and the International Bank for Reconstruction and Development shall be the international entity entrusted with the operation of the financial mechanism referred to in Article 11 on an interim basis. In this connection, the Global Environment Facility should be appropriately restructured and its membership made universal to enable it to fulfill the requirements of Article 11.

ARTICLE 22 — RATIFICATION, ACCEPTANCE, APPROVAL OR ACCESSION

1. The Convention shall be subject to ratification, acceptance, approval or accession by States and by regional economic integration organizations. It shall be open for accession from the day after the date on which the Convention is closed for signature. Instruments of ratification, acceptance, approval or accession shall be deposited with the Depositary.

2. Any regional economic integration organization which becomes a Party to the Convention without any of its member States being a Party shall be bound by all the obligations under the Convention. In the case of such organizations, one or more of whose member States is a Party to the Convention, the organization and its member States shall decide on their respective responsibilities for the performance of their obligations under the Convention. In such cases, the organization and the member States shall not be entitled to exercise rights under the Convention concurrently.

3. In their instruments of ratification, acceptance, approval or accession, regional economic integration organizations shall declare the extent of their competence with respect to the

matters governed by the Convention. These organizations shall also inform the Depositary, who shall in turn inform the Parties, of any substantial modification in the extent of their competence.

ARTICLE 23 — ENTRY INTO FORCE

1. The Convention shall enter into force on the ninetieth day after the date of deposit of the fiftieth instrument of ratification, acceptance, approval or accession.

2. For each State or regional economic integration organization that ratifies, accepts or approves the Convention or accedes thereto after the deposit of the fiftieth instrument of ratification, acceptance, approval or accession, the Convention shall enter into force on the ninetieth day after the date of deposit by such State or regional economic integration organization of its instrument of ratification, acceptance, approval or accession.

3. For the purposes of paragraphs 1 and 2 above, any instrument deposited by a regional economic integration organization shall not be counted as additional to those deposited by States members of the organization.

ARTICLE 24 — RESERVATIONS

No reservations may be made to the Convention.

Text of UNFCCC Treaty

ARTICLE 25 — WITHDRAWAL

[XXII] 1. *At any time after three years from the date on which the Convention has entered into force for a Party, that Party may withdraw from the Convention by giving written notification to the Depositary.*

2. *Any such withdrawal shall take effect upon expiry of one year from the date of receipt by the Depositary of the notification of withdrawal,* or on such later date as may be specified in the notification of withdrawal.

3. *Any Party that withdraws from the Convention shall be considered as also having withdrawn from any protocol to which it is a Party.*

ARTICLE 26 — AUTHENTIC TEXTS

The original of this Convention, of which the Arabic, Chinese, English, French, Russian and Spanish texts are equally authentic, shall be deposited with the Secretary-General of the United Nations.

IN WITNESS WHEREOF the undersigned, being duly authorized to that effect, have signed this Convention.

DONE at New York this ninth day of May one thousand nine hundred and ninety-two.

Annex I

Australia

Austria

Belarus*

Text of UNFCCC Treaty

Belgium

Bulgaria*

Canada

Czechoslovakia*

Denmark

European Economic Community

Estonia*

Finland

France

Germany

Greece

Hungary*

Iceland

Ireland

Italy

Japan

Latvia*

Lithuania*

Luxembourg

Netherlands

New Zealand

Norway

Text of UNFCCC Treaty

Poland*

Portugal

Romania*

Russian Federation

Spain

Sweden

Switzerland

Turkey

Ukraine*

United Kingdom of Great Britain and Northern Ireland

United States of America

* Countries that are undergoing the process of transition to a
  market economy.

<u>Annex II</u>

Australia

Austria

Belgium

Canada

Denmark

European Economic Community

Finland

France

Text of UNFCCC Treaty

Germany

Greece

Iceland

Ireland

Italy

Japan

Luxembourg

Netherlands

New Zealand

Norway

Portugal

Spain

Sweden

Switzerland

Turkey

United Kingdom of Great Britain and Northern Ireland

United States of America

NOTES

Summary COP 21 Agreement. http://bigpicture.unfccc.int/
#content-the-paris-agreement.

ibid.

Economist magazine, November 18, 2015

"Presidential Climate Action Project, Questions and Answers
Emissions Reductions Needed to Stabilize Climate," by Susan
Joy Hassol, for the Presidential Climate Action Project. http://
bit.ly/2jVcQP9

The Guardian, November 19, 2014, Arthur Neslen, Brussels,
reporting on the United Nations Environment Program Report.

National Geographic, "According to the IPCC, we'd have to
reduce GHG emissions by 50% to 80%." http://on.natgeo.com/
2jH29SI

"Energy Secretary Optimistic on Obama's Plan to Reduce
Emissions", by Matthew L. Wald, *New York Times*, June 27,
2013. http://nyti.ms/2kaOuo8

Forbes, "The Alarming Cost Of Climate Change Hysteria,"
Larry Bell, August 23, 2011. http://bit.ly/2kb8AP5

"Federal Climate Change Expenditures Report" to Congress,
Table 1, August, 2013.

0. *Economist* magazine, "The deepest cuts" September 20, 2014.
http://econ.st/2jIgqPv

1. EPA http://bit.ly/2jGJTc6 EPA currently combines gasoline and
other fuels into a single transportation category. Emissions
from electricity generation and transportation combined

represented 56% of total CO2 emissions in 2014.

12. *"Powering Africa,"* byAntonio Castellano, Adam Kendall, Mikhail Nikomarov, and Tarryn Swemmer, February, 2015. http://bit.ly/2j2Ym1t

13. This practice began with the Kyoto protocol.

14. This ignores forecast growth in demand of approximately 1% annually, between now and 2050. It also ignores any reductions in demand through energy savings. In essence, it assumes that demand growth will be offset by energy savings.

    It also ignores the projected decline of nuclear power by 2050, which increases the difficulty of lowering CO2 emissions, while increasing the amount of wind and solar required.

15. Calculation for number of 2MW wind turbines.

    Capacity Factor (CF) = 30%, multiplied times 2 Megawatts (MW) equals 600 Kilowatts, times hours in year = 5,256,000 kWh per year.

    The lost coal and natural gas generating capacity of 441,704 MW, with an average CF of 0.8, results in lost output of 3,095,461,632 MWh or 3,095,461,632,000 kWh per year.

    Total kWh of lost output divided by 5,256,000 = 588,939 new wind turbines rated 2M. With a cost of $2,000,000 each, total cost would be $1,177,877,833.

    Using a capacity factor of 0.2, the cost for PV solar would be approximately $2.0 trillion.

16. "The Joint Coordinated System Plan" (JCSP) study covered less than half the United States, and was for wind to only

NOTES

achieve 20% penetration. The amount of wind and solar required to replace coal-fired and natural gas power generation across the U.S. is far greater than the amount of wind and solar necessary to achieve 20% penetration in the Eastern United States.

JCSP was produced with the collaborative efforts of Midwest ISO, Southwest Power Pool, Inc., PJM Interconnection, the Tennessee Valley Authority, Mid-Continent Area Power Pool, and participants within SERC Reliability Corp. http://bit.ly/2j3qp0s

7. The combined Capacity Factor for the coal and natural gas power plants removed from service would be approximately 80%. Using a Capacity Factor of 90% for nuclear would result in approximately 400 new power plants being required.

8. "Ethanol: Higher Emissions or Lower?" by Brooks Jackson, November 23, 2015. http://bit.ly/2jIorDW

9. Portions of this appendix have been drawn from *Nothing to Fear,* by the author, January 1, 2016. ISBN 978-0-9815119-2-4

20. *ibid.*

21. PNNL.gov 2009, "Future CO2 Pipelines Not as Onerous as Some Think." http://1.usa.gov/1IQz11h

22. European Commission, Joint Research Center, "The evolution of the extent and the investment requirements of a trans-European CO2 transport network," by Joris Morbee, Joana Serpa, Evangelos Tzimas. http://bit.ly/2jy2ViV

NOTES

23. *"Nano-spike catalysts convert carbon dioxide directly into ethanol,"* Morgan McCorkle, Oak Ridge National Laboratory, October 12. 2016. http://bit.ly/2k9siXg

24. The inference is that it makes little sense to build wind farms merely to generate electricity for producing ethanol.

25. *"Turning greenhouse gas into gasoline,"* David L. Chandler, MIT News Office, November 15, 2016. http://bit.ly/2iKKOc9

26. Consolidated Edison's proposed pumped storage at Storm King Mountain, along the Hudson River was abandoned in 1962 due to opposition by environmental groups. http://on.ny.gov/2iKK86W

27. National Hydropower Association, "Hydro Works for America." http://bit.ly/2jgQSpm

28. CAISO Battery Storage Trial, Nov 21, 2016, by Todd Kiefer in *The Grid Optimization Blog.* http://bit.ly/2iKSrPY

29. Ultra-supercritical (USC) coal-fired power plants operate at very high temperatures and pressures. While the existing fleet of coal-fired power plants in the United States operate at 32% efficiency based on the higher heating value (HHV) of the coal, USC plants can operate at 46% HHV efficiency. This represents an approximate 44% improvement in efficiency. http://bit.ly/2jhcsd6

About The Author

Donn Dears began his career at General Electric testing large steam turbines and generators used by utilities to generate electricity; followed next, by manufacturing and marketing assignments at the Transformer Division. He led an organization of a few thousand people servicing these and other GE products in the United States. He then established facilities around the world to service power generation, transmission equipment and other electric apparatus. Later, he led an engineering department of several hundred people that provided engineering support to nearly a hundred service installations around the world.

At nearly every step, Donn was involved with the work done at customer locations: at steel mills, electric utilities, refineries, oil drilling and production facilities and open pit and underground mining operations. At every opportunity, he learned of the needs of these industries.

Donn has had a close-up view of the eastern province of Saudi Arabia with its oil producing and shipping facilities. He has investigated many of the other oil producing countries in the Mideast and Northern Europe, as well as examining iron-ore mining locations and major shipping centers in Europe and Asia. All told, Donn has visited over 50 countries and has knowledge of their need for the technologies that can improve their well being and their use of equipment manufactured in the United States.

Following his retirement as a senior GE Company executive, he continued to study and write about energy issues.

Donn is a graduate of the United States Merchant Marine Academy and served on active duty in the U.S. Navy.

Index

Africa, 16, 18, 60, 94

Algeria, 39

Aliso Canyon, 40

Annex I, 61, 64, 65, 78, 89

Annex II, 64, 65, 78, 91

anthropogenic, 5, 56, 57, 59,
61-63, 65, 77, 78

Asia, 16, 97

baseload, 21

Canada, 39, 90, 91

carbon capture and
sequestration (CCS), 20, 37, 39,
40

China, 1, 13, 14, 16, 17, 33

Clexit, 1, 5

climate change, 1, 3, 5, 7, 8, 10,
16, 18, 33, 34, 42, 51-55,
57-61, 63, 65-70, 74-76,
86, 93

coal, 19, 21, 38, 94-96

coal-fired power plants, 18,
20-23, 25-27, 37, 38, 42,
96

coal-fired, ultra-supercritical
power plants (USC), 48, 96

CO2, 20,27,29,37,38-43, 95

CO2, Atmospheric, 7, 13, 37,
42

CO2, Emissions, 5,7-11, 13-20,
22, 25, 27-34, 37, 94

Conference of the Parties, 1, 5,
7, 57, 59, 61-66, 69-77,
79-82, 85, 86

conciliation commission, 82

Connecticut Light and Power,
45

COP 21,1, 7, 8, 10, 15, 33, 93

COP 22, 16

Crescent Dunes Concentrating
Solar Plant, 46

Earth, 33, 51

Economist Magazine, 8, 10, 93

electric vehicles, 2, 25, 26

enhanced oil recovery (EOR),
39

EPA, 9, 19, 20, 93

ethanol, 20, 25, 41, 42, 95, 96

EU28, 14, 16

Europe, 14, 16, 17, 39, 97

Federal Climate Change
Expenditures Report to
Congress, 10

financial mechanism, 75-77, 87

financial resources, 31, 64, 65,
71, 75, 77, 79

fossil fuel(s), 2, 45, 54, 66, 67

fuel cells, 2, 25, 27

Index

gasoline, 2, 13-15, 19, 25-30, 41, 42, 93, 96

General Assembly Resolutions, 53

Germany, 11, 45, 90, 92

Global Warming Pollution Reduction Act, 9

Green Climate Fund, 34

greenhouse effect, 54

greenhouse gases (GHG), 1, 5, 8, 15, 32, 33, 51, 54-63, 65, 70, 78, 93, 96

Huntorf, Germany, 45

Hutchison, Kansas, 40

hydrogen, 27,28,38

hydropower, 19, 45

India, 1, 14, 16, 17

integrated gasification combined cycle (IGCC), 38, 40

Intergovernmental Panel on Climate Change (IPCC), 15, 86, 93

International Atomic Energy Agency, 72, 86

International Bank for Reconstruction, 87

International Court of Justice, 35, 81

Iran, 35

Japan, 14, 16, 17, 90, 92

Liberty County, Texas, 40

Marrakesh, 16

McKinsey & Company, 18

McIntosh, Alabama, 45

methane, 27

methane reforming, 27, 28

MIT, 17, 42, 96

Montreal Protocol, 53, 59-62, 64, 65, 77

National Geographic Magazine, 9, 93

Nothing to Fear, 5, 30, 95

Norway, 39, 90, 92

nuclear, 2, 19, 22, 23, 38, 47-49, 94, 95

nuclear operating license, 47

Oakridge National Laboratory, 41, 96

Obama, President, 1, 7, 9, 19, 34, 93

Pacific Northwest National Laboratory (PNNL), 26, 39

Paris Accord/Agreement, 1, 7, 16, 33, 93

per capita emissions, 14, 31, 51

photovoltaic (PV), 22, 94

pipelines, 39,95

precautionary, 32, 58

Index

Russia, 13, 14, 16, 17

Second World Climate
Conference, 53

Sleipner oil field, 39

solar, 2, 20-22, 41, 42, 46, 94,
95

South Korea, 16

Statoil, 39

Stockholm, 52

Subsidiary Body for
Implementation (SBI),7, 75

Subsidiary Body for Scientific
and Technological Advice
(SBSTA) 8, 73

storage, 22, 28, 40, 45, 46, 49

storage, compressed air energy
(CAES), 45, 46

storage, battery, 96

storage, pumped, 45, 46, 96

storage, thermal, 46

United Nations (UN), 1, 3, 16,
51-53, 72, 86, 89

United Nations Environment
Program, 53, 93

United Nations Framework
Convention on Climate Change
(UNFCCC) 1, 3, 5, 7, 9, 10, 15,
31-36, 51

UNFCCC Treaty Text,
Highlighted, [I] 51,
[II] 52,
[III] 57,

(continued)
[IV] 58,
[V] 59,
[VI] 59,
[VII] 61,
[VIII] 61,
[IX] 62,
[X] 64,
[XI] 68,
[XII] 69,
[XIII] 71,
[XIV] 71,
[XV] 72,
[XVI] 73,
[XVII] 75,
[XVIII] 77,
[XIX] 80,
[XX] 82,
[XXI] 85,
[XXII] 89

vehicles, battery powered,
25-27, 29

vehicles, electric, 2, 25, 26

vehicles, light, 25, 26, 29

wind, 2, 20-22, 41, 42, 46,
94-96

withdrawal, 36, 84, 89

World Meteorological
Organization, 53

Yucca Mountain, 49

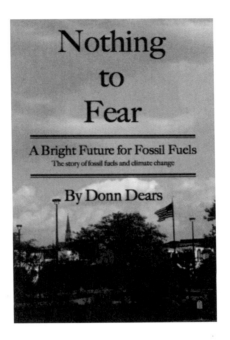

Obtain a copy of *Nothing to Fear* at the special price of

$8.00

by cutting out and mailing this page to:

The Heartland Institute
Attn. Publications Department
3939 North Wilke Road
Arlington Heights, Illinois 60004

(Make check payable to The Heartland Institute.)